TREES:
An Alphabet

Trees: An Alphabet

This edition documents the publication of Trees: An Alphabet: 26 poems by Philip Sharpe and 26 hand-cut, relief prints by Andrew Judd. The original work was printed letterpress and from the relief blocks by Evergreen Press in a limited edition of 26 sale copies and published by MKB Editions.

Text © Philip Sharpe
Illustrations © Andrew Judd

ISBN 13: 978-0-9555872-1-4

Digitally printed on 100gsm Stow Book wove by:

Aspect Design
89 Newtown Road
Malvern
Worcestershire
WR14 1PD

Published by:

MKB Editions
345 Kings Acre Road
Hereford
HR4 0SL

TREES:
An Alphabet

Poems by Philip Sharpe
Prints by Andrew Judd

MKB EDITIONS 2007

And he looked up, and said, I see men as trees, walking.

St Mark Ch. 8 v. 24

mi ritrovai per una selva oscura

Dante, Inferno Canto I

TREES: AN ALPHABET

Ash

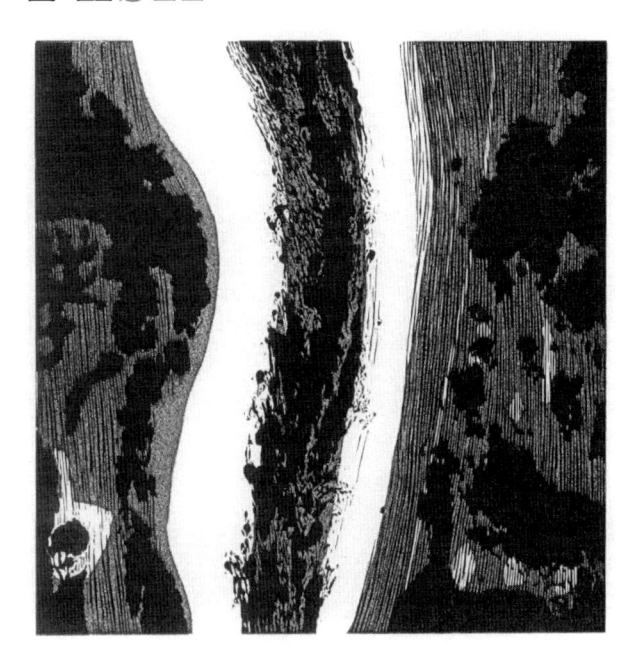

as
smoke
happens

Box

edging a garden,
containing earth

Copse

grown for the fire, fuelling
the sun on plough's grate
this late evening, frail
and distinct, before the light goes,
before the fire comes

Dendrophobia

in dark woods
we see ourselves

Elder

soft shoots soon harden,
soon bear dark fruit

Fire

however long life,
a quick consumption

Gibbet

we can't let things be –
on a gamekeeper's gibbet
countless squirrels, hollow
and dry as dead sticks,
flute the wind –
man makes his music

Haft

in this shapeless world
something turned,
to get hold of

Ivy-bush

imbosked in an ale-stake's shade
we drink to dryads, again,
again

Judas-tree

fruit hung, betrayed
by being

Kindling

life transforms –
twigs blacken into ash,
into charcoal

Leaf

once felled man's still;
but moved by unseen winds
leaves fall, and rise –
hold this page with care

Mistletoe

clinging in love
we live off each other,
forget the birdlime
in lingering kisses

Nut

love rots into life –
from sweet moments
come monstrous growths

Osmosis

we can't be kept apart –
earth will accommodate us,
come, my frail love

Pleach

a hedge well-laid –
man, made nature

Quickbeam

'i see men as trees,'
inspired, alive,
cut by runes

Ring

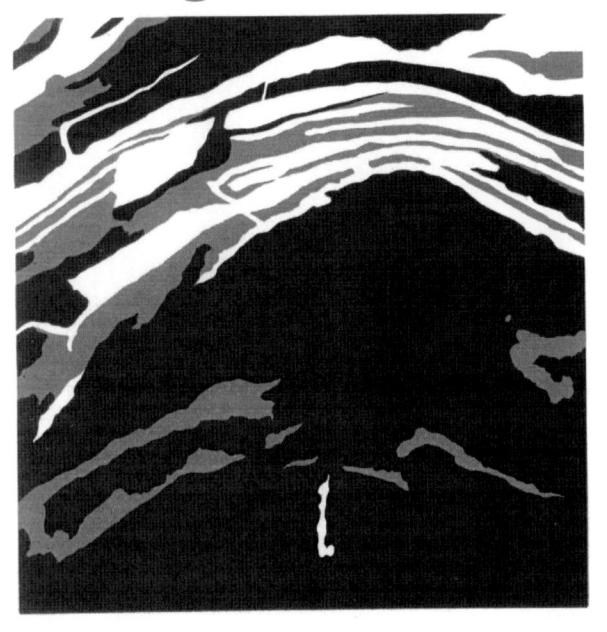

through the bole,
a seed's ripples

Stump

lopped, alive,
all possibilities gone

Twig

a bronchiole, each tree a lung –
a deep breath in the lightest breeze

Umbrage

we seek ease in change –
welcome shade, welcome
the sun

Vallombrosa

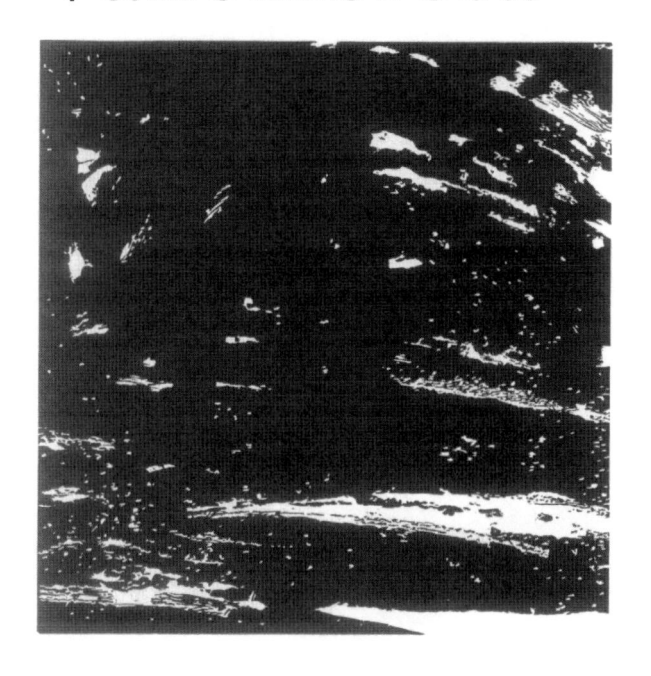

walking on through it
fearing all things –
light; each falling leaf

Walking stick

needing support, we
move by amputations

X

a cross, bearing
scattered limbs

Yew

i think of you, a shade
before darker shades

z

in this dark place, sounds
cut perfect silence

zzzzzzzzzzz

living wood / dead wood